the
nature
of
self love

A little book of akashic wisdom—written by Laura Coe;
Guided by the Akashic Records.

LAURA COE

Dedication

Thankfully, the universe spoke, and I listened.

Then love spoke, and I kept listening.

Introduction

This is a story about love. This is a story about a return to love. A return to self-love and a return to the joy that lay dormant, in need of resurrection. This is my story, told in part by me and in part by the energy that surrounds all of us. Some people may refer to that energy field as Akasha, and some may refer to it as the energy of light or source. Others may experience it as God. For me, it is less about what we call it and more about what we can do with it; how it impacts our soul's journey, our learning, and our essence.

This energy surrounds all of us and all of us can access it and do access it without awareness. It is the energy that suggests you contact a friend in need out of nowhere; it is the energy that guides your decisions – be it a call to a purpose, a love, a change of location or a change of heart.

It is that which guides us from deep within but it is not solely within. It is around; it is everywhere and it is nowhere. It is like the air. It is in my lungs and in the world, and in your lungs. It cannot be contained as one thing, and yet it is one thing: air. And that is you. You are like the air. You are nowhere and everywhere. You are in the physical, like the air comes into the lungs and is in the physical body, and you are non-physical, like the air surrounding you. And this paradox is the key to unlock your joy. It is in the knowing that we are both the physical manifestation of energy and, at the same time, the energy that surrounds us. There is then no beginning and no end to any one of us, or to anything.

This is my story. This is the story that was shared through me when I learned to connect to this energy field, as you can, as anyone can. This is my story into love, into my heart, into my true knowing of who I am. While I studied, wrote, blogged, podcasted, and taught on the true meaning of authenticity for a decade, I did not unlock the timeless nature and beauty of it until I understood the nature of our soul, our soul's journey, and the interconnected nature of all things.

I wish to take you on this journey with me, into the energy, the akasha, into the light that surrounds us and is us. I wish to take you with me on that journey so that you may too choose to unlock this field of light and join me and countless souls who have done the same. I am not a mystic and I am able to access this field of light. And so, it is my belief that the world will be a safer, happier, and a more joyous place if we can all unlock this energetic space for guidance into our potential. Most of us look to our achievements, to our relationships, to our mothers or fathers or even to a higher power source we hope surrounds us for answers. But our potential can be seen in an instant when we experience the light field that surrounds all of us.

And know it is available to all of us, and is us.

I wrote each lesson in this series to help me heal: heal my heartbreak, heal my unresolved emotions, even heal my life's melodramas. Each lesson led me one step further down my path because it was in the lessons that I moved deeper into my truth, into my authentic self, and towards my destiny. I learned we enter into divine motion, not when we achieve more, but when we unlock the next lesson in our soul's journey.

We are all able to experience ecstatic joy, and we are all the same in our desires to find love, meaning, and freedom: The freedom to be exactly who we are and where we are in every moment, despite the difficulties we may face. Because it is not in the overcoming of these difficulties that we truly experience joy, it is in the surrender that we find joy. It is in the surrender into the simplicity that we are already capable of endless love, endless joy, and endless happiness. We do not have to change, make more, do more, or be more. We can experience any state we desire, even when our surroundings suggest we should feel differently.

This is my story into the Akasha, into the light that is always ever-present. And this is a story into my heart, and the details of my journey with my soulmate. Yes, I found my soulmate in this life, and not just any soulmate, I found my twin flame. And

I, like a Hollywood movie, fell head over heels in love, as did she. And like a twin flame love can, we found that our love transcended logic, personal agendas, and just about any rationale that previously guided our decisions. We were in love and our love moved us to transform, to break down, to show up new and to decide ultimately if love would prevail.

And it was in this love that I found my way back to my truth - the truth that I am a writer. That I am a spiritual seeker. That I am on a path towards my destiny that I and only I hold the key to unlock my truth in this lifetime and lives to follow. And it was in love that I found the beauty, not of soulmate love, but of myself. And it was in love that I found that love of self was more important than any other love, any other motive, and any other agenda. As it seems that when you find love of your self, love of the person you choose to be in this lifetime, and you allow her to show up as she alone knows she is meant to, that all else fades into nothingness. It is not about fighting for your freedom to be in your truth with others, but it is about fighting for your freedom to show up to your self without hate, without fear, without arresting who you are for an idea of who you should be.

And it was in that love that I really understood how to let go. How to let love leave if it was not meant to be and flow when it is meant to. And if it is not given back, I still can give my love to myself. And if it is not taken care of, I can still love. And if I am harmed, I can always forgive, for it is in my nature to let the rivers of love continue to flow. And if I am sad or anxious or lost or lonely, I can always find my way back by knowing I am loved. I am love. We are all love. We are all made of the same fabric and just as we inhale and exhale until we take our last breath, we can allow the love within to flow just as easily.

So, I hope that you enjoy the lessons I learned and how I share them with you through the connection to the energy field of the Akasha. And more than that, I hope that you find the joy within, that you find the flow of love within you, and that you offer that love to yourself and to everyone surrounding you. And I hope that when and if that love is not reciprocated, you never stop loving yourself and others. And if you find you must walk away from love, never walk away from the love of your self. And finally, I hope you open your self to the light in whatever ways you can in all ways you can, and as often as you can.

With love,
Laura and the guided light energy of the Akasha.

the
nature
of
self love

Imagine a lion standing amongst the tall grasses

    deep within the savanna.

Imagine brightly lit green grass rests as

    far as the eye can see,

    less one lion's head propped up staring without agenda.

Imagine flies move across his view,

    grasses wave gracefully with the changing winds,

    and only the sounds of nature's calling

    make up the rest of his day.

He sits.

He waits for nothing,

as he has just fed and his belly is full.

His face is without intention

as he has nothing to attend to.

He simply sits and watches over the fields

he does not call home;

the home of a lion is every moment

he finds himself sitting in.

His life is made up of nothingness.

He needs nothing.

He desires nothing.

He simply sits in the field or wanders without cause.

When he rises to walk about,

he thinks of no plan,

he wonders of no failures,

he does not question his nature

or the meaning of his existence.

He waits.

He sits.

He hunts.

And when he succeeds, he feeds.

And when he fails, he returns to stillness.

And when he has completed what amounts to nothing,

he sleeps without a sense of time.

He sleeps to rest and

when he wakes

he is not reminded of

his past failures or his future concerns.

He simply returns to the present.

In a bush sits a man.

This man has come from faraway lands to the same field,
but this man has not come with the same task.
He has not come to sit, sleep, and rest without agenda.

He has come to kill.

He has come to find this lion
to connect to and establish his personal power.

As he watches the lion,

he lifts binoculars up to his face

and observes this lion

sitting in the middle of the grasses.

He wonders if this lion is indeed stronger

    and more significant than he.

He wonders about the lion's time spent

    and how the lion makes his next move.

He wonders about what the lion may be reflecting on

    and imagines the lion contemplating revenge

    for an act committed on his family

    by a nearby pack of lions.

He wonders about the lion's dreams

    and wanderings

    and he asks himself in his notebooks at night

    if the lion knows of what he does.

He remarks to himself of the lion's

comings and goings,

dreams and wishes,

and he asks himself what if anything they might mean.

As he scratches his pencil into his paper

he tires slowly until he drifts into sleep.

He knows that the day is coming when he will face his fears

and capture or kill this lion,

prove his prowess,

and return home a king of kings amongst men of men.

As the man drifts off to sleep,

he forgets to put out the remains of his fire that

crackles gently as he loses consciousness.

Deep asleep, the man dreams of his lion.

He dreams of the moment

he takes his dagger out of the lion's heart,

stands tall,

foot on the lion's belly,

victorious over his prey.

As he dreams of his victory,
he is unaware of the silent breath standing above him.
He is unaware of the change of smell and temperature.

His eyes pop open to find not
the lion he wishes to defeat,
but instead the lion that will find peace
in having located his next meal.

And in an instant,

without thought,

without care,

without agenda,

the lion lifts his paw

and slaps it across the man's face,

leaving lines never to be forgotten.

Blood dripping,

the lion moves closer,

takes another piece of the man's face,

not for the joy of the hunt,

but simply due to the instinct to kill.

Again, without thought, the lion moves in for his final blow.

The man looks up at his fate

and wonders how he has found such an

unfortunate outcome,

just as the lion opens his mouth,

teeth exposed,

ready to kill.

The man pauses

and watches the lion

with the same interest he had

as he watched his then prey in the field,

and he wonders again,

not of his own fate

- which seems determined -

but of his own intention.

And in that instant,

        as he meets his death,

                he realizes the meaning of self-love.

The man learned in wondering of another,

he lost focus on himself.

And in that lost focus,

he lost his life.

He was so lost in the comings and goings of the lion,

that he did not notice his own destiny was being

determined by his failure

to stand watch over his own life.

The man need not know why the lion

was sitting in the tall grass.

He need not know why the lion

rests or sits in the winds.

He need not know why the lion

wished to sit without purpose.

The man only needed to know why he travelled across

the lands to find this lion,

hunt this lion,

and in so doing restore what he believed

was his own purpose when,

in fact,

he only watched this lion living.

He only needed to know why

    he wished to watch this lion.

He only needed to know what

    drew him into the lion's den

    wondering what the lion wondered about.

He only needed to know that

    the lion never wondered about him

    and he needed not wonder of the lion.

He needed not to sit in a field

to study the lion who he wished

to hunt and kill for fame and fortune,

but only to wonder why

he wished for that fame and fortune.

When the man sat in the field and faced his death

he knew that the lion and he were the same,

but that the lion lived as he should:

as a lion.

The man had not lived as a man.

He had lived as an impostor.

He spent his time in search,

in far lands,

looking for his purpose.

While the man searched for his destiny,

the lion lived in his destiny with each step,

each breath, and each moment.

The man realized in his final breath that he,

like the lion,

was meant to live in harmony,

in the fields of his dreams,

without a desire to be elsewhere

or to ponder the doings of others at the expense

of his own destiny.

Self-love,

the love of self,

the love of who we are and why we are here,

is not found in faraway lands

or in search of another,

or through the study of the path

that was not designed for you.

The lion lived as a lion.

The man lived as a man
considering the life of a lion.

Self-love is found in the simplicity of looking within,

pencil in hand,

and reflecting on why you are standing in a field,

why you are gazing on a lion,

and why you are drawn to conquer another.

Self-love is to know that your path

is not in the admiration of another,

the defeat of another,

the loss of self in another in a faraway land.

Self-love is only found when you know the truth

of why you were born

and what you have come to accomplish.

When you love yourself,

when you practice self-love,

you sit in the fields of your own life

and you need not ponder your purpose;

you know your purpose.

When you practice self-love,

you need not know the meaning of your next move;

you are in the presence of your current move.

You need not hunt other's actions for answers

or inflate your sense of self through their failures;

you can find your worth in knowing

you are doing exactly what you are meant to do.

The lion knows his purpose and position.

He does what he was born to do.

When you chase after answers in faraway fields

in hopes you will find your purpose

over a fire in your journal at night,

you will most certainly find your end.

You will find you are alone

and with no more information

than the beauty of the field in which you reside.

Self-love is to know who you are does not require travel,

    prowess, journals or pursuit of others.

Self-love requires us to trust that we are not a mistake.

    We are not born imperfect,

    flawed, or without purpose.

Self-love is to believe in yourself

    with the same vigor that you believe in others.

Self-love is to know that your value is not in question.

    Your existence is not without meaning.

And you and you alone have the key to unlock

the meaning that already exists within.

No one can do that for you.

They can light the path,

they can ignite your soul,

they can give a warm embrace when you are feeling low,

but you alone can find the essence

of who you are and why you are here.

And that does not take a battle,

a search across lands.

Find the person you
without question know has internal beauty,
you believe in fully,
and then know that you are just as worthy
of such praise and belief.

When you can wish the greatest dreams upon yourself,

when you can believe in your fullest potential

    even when you fall,

when you can see your light,

    even when it is dim,

        then you have found what you seek.

The man lies in the field

and awaits the fame he seeks,

he waits for the approval that is to come,

he hunts for the meaning in the lion's activities and

wonders of his own importance

in the happenings of the lion.

The lion simply lives.
The lion simply follows his truth.

The lion knows his own path
and moves without thought.

The man knows not what he wants
other than fame and fortune
and to win over the lion in the field.

This is not self-love.

This is not living in one's truth.

This is living in the presence of another,

seeking truth outside of where the truth resides.

Truth resides within.

The truth you seek is the truth in your heart.

The lion lives without the madness of the mind

suggesting he is anything other than himself.

The man listens to the mind telling him that

the life of a lion will lead him to a life he can call his own.

The man's heart cannot speak when it is covered
in the lies of the mind that suggests he is not enough.

His heart cannot locate the truth that it desires
when the heaviness of the mind overwhelms its power.

The mind

wishes to conquer.

The mind

wants fame and fortune.

The heart

simply lives to find the truth

that easily flows through

and out into the world

without awareness of the outcomes.

So the practice of self-love requires

knowing what is in your heart.

And to know your heart,

you must be able to access its strength,

as the heart knows who you are,

why you are here,

and that you are always enough.

But when you doubt who you are,

and whether you are truly enough,

you can always come back to the heart

by returning to love.

By allowing love to flow through you,

you will open up the heart's song,

allowing it to sing your truth more freely.

Begin with love.

Begin with locating the love you have

    for that which brings you joy.

Begin to locate all things that uplift the heart.

In each act that lifts the heart towards its truth,

the heartbeat will remind you of your purpose

and will lead you down your path towards your destiny.

By finding what brings you joy,

you will begin to ignite the power of the heart

against the mental obstacles

that suggest your joy is not the joy you seek.

The knowing in the heart's center is the simplest path

to living in one's truth.

Self-love,

the love of self,

is to rise up to our purpose

over the purpose of another because

we can find our truth.

We wish,

like the man in the field who watches the lion,

to conquer what is not for us to conquer.

Look inside and learn to love what is you,

what you love,

what ignites your spirit,

and be in the practice of only following that truth.

Like the lion,

wake and sleep in the bliss

of being exactly who you are.

Self-love,

love of self,

is to love exactly what makes you you.

And only attempt to be you,

and to love that for the simplicity that it is enough.

Love moves through us like a river
keeping us in a state of harmony,
but self-love is the guide to our path.

It is the internal light
– the light of knowing who we are -
and in the acceptance that
moves us on the journey towards our destiny
of that we alone can navigate.

Seek guidance,

seek support,

but only you and you alone can know if the path

you walk is aligned with your self.

Love that,

and all will be well.